Calisthenics 101: Everything You Need to Know About Bodyweight Exercising

Talha Erol

Talha Erol

Disclaimer

All erudition contained in this book is given for informational and educational purposes only. The author is not in any way accountable for any results or outcomes that emanate from using this material. Constructive attempts have been made to provide information that is both accurate and effective, but the author is not bound for the accuracy or use/misuse of this information.

Table of Contents

Introduction

Life is about where you are right now, and the choices you make. – Cory Booker

For decades, we have considered the modern-day gym and equipment therein to be the most natural way to go about exercising and engaging our bodies. Everyone you know probably has some kind of gym membership, which is why you feel like you should have one, too. It has become something that is commonplace, and for many people, the gym has become a place of mental respite where they can unplug from the world around them and just let go.

However, as COVID-19 arrived in 2020, gyms have closed their doors – some of them worry it will be a permanent change. Gyms present themselves as a potential for massive germ dissemination as multiple people, per day, touch the same knobs, levers, and weights, sweating all over the equipment. With something as serious as coronavirus, societies can't take that risk right now.

That has put the worldwide population at home, wondering how they are going to work out. If you've been accustomed to using the same machines, day after day, at the gym, what are you going to do right now? Believe it or not, you don't need those machines. In fact, you don't need that gym membership either. All you need is some space and your body. That's it.

Calisthenics is an ancient bodyweight training method in which the human body, its inertia, and the natural gravity enacted on the body are used to build muscle, lose weight, and tone the body. In this form of training, all you need is your human, breathing body, and the ability to jump, squat, roll and push. That's it.

Post-COVID-19 World: A New Dawn for Calisthenics?

If you are reading this e-book today, then you want to know more about Calisthenics. You want to know what it entails, what you need to do it correctly, how to perform the bodyweight exercises correctly, how to eat a diet that matches your exercise, and how to create the perfect workout plan for where you are physically. You know that we might not be able to go back to gyms for a year or more right now, which is why you want to get in control of your physical health and form right at home.

Calisthenics provides you with that personal freedom and autonomy over your body – something you might not have previously had. As society slowly goes back to normal over the next few years, your understanding of Calisthenics is something that can't be taken away from you. In fact, understanding your body with such clarity and acceptance will align your mind, body, and soul more than ever before. You'll witness benefits that extend well beyond simple physical fitness and a lean physique.

There's a reason calisthenics were used by ancient Greek Olympians, and are still used to train the strength and gymnast Olympians today in 2020. It's a natural form of exercise that just can't be wavered, even in the midst of a global pandemic.

Therefore, in this e-book, we are going to cover everything you need to know about Calisthenics. We are going to look at the basics, the perfect execution when it comes to Calisthenics, how to adjust your nutrition, how to find routines that work for you, what kind of equipment you can add to the mix, and finally, the perfect workout plan, made with your physical experience in mind.

It's time to learn more about something so innate and natural for the human body. It's time to adapt to this "new normal" in a work-from-home world. Just because you are staying at home every day now, doesn't mean you shouldn't be exercising and engaging your body. Exercise has been proven to engage the brain, support new brain cell growth, and even aid in memory recall.

So without further ado, it's time to dive into the world of Calisthenics.

Chapter 1: What is Calisthenics?

In order to benefit to the greatest extent from this e-book guide, you need to first understand what Calisthenics is, what it isn't, what it can offer you, as well as what it can't offer you today. Before we dive into the details, let's take a little walk down through history.

Calisthenics is derived from the ancient Greek word "kallos," which means beauty, and "sthenos," which means strength. When you put those two together, it can be thought of as creating art using nothing but your own body weight, inertia, and gravity to develop your physical physique.

Calisthenics can be traced back to the dawn of human evolution, where humans had to walk, run, jump, lunge, roll, and pull to merely stay alive. In fact, modern gym equipment has been modeled after this kind of survival techniques to engage those muscle groups around your body. That is why Calisthenics is often regarded as "the most natural and comfortable type of exercise" for the human body to perform. Even homo sapiens cousins, like the monkey or ape, use this kind of exercise to develop their arm, chest, and back muscles.

During these ancient times, Calisthenics was also used as the main source of physical training for militias, armies, and soldiers. It was the most effective way to train men while also teaching them to organize, collect, and work together physically. There has always been something spiritual not only when it comes to being aware of your body, but also enduring that kind of awareness with other people.

Bodyweight exercising with slow, purposeful muscle engagement, and enhanced flexibility, over time, gave rise to the most well-known master of Calisthenics today: the gymnast. Beyond lifting heavy weights or running miles, many gymnasts train 30-40 hours per week using nothing but their own bodyweight, inertia, and purposeful movement.

Thanks to technology and the dissemination of gymnastics competitions globally, as well as through the Olympics, this form of working out has gained new popularity. Social media stars are providing more content regarding their workout regimes, shedding light on Calisthenics, and how valuable this kind of exercise can be for the body. Plus, Calisthenics are the easiest workout "forms" athletes can film and share on social media since it does not require: equipment, gym memberships, or class memberships. Anyone can do it, right at home, and follow along with their videos.

Wikipedia provides the following calisthenics definition: "Calisthenics is a form of exercise consisting of a variety of gross motor movements, like standing, pushing, or running, often performed rhythmically and with minimal equipment, as a bodyweight exercise. They are intended to increase strength, fitness, and flexibility, through pulling, jumping, squatting, swinging, and doing anything else that engages your innate bodyweight. Calisthenics can provide the benefits of muscular and aerobic conditioning, in addition to improving psychomotor skills like balance, agility, and coordination."

At its core, Calisthenics is the most natural, pure form of exercise, one that people have been doing for thousands of years. It's not about fancy equipment, gym memberships, or specialized classes. It's about taking your body and moving it through intentional bursts, jumps, runs, or squats to engage different muscle groups for strength conditioning, weight loss, agility enhancement, and so forth.

Since Calisthenics is so innate to humans as a workout method, sports teams, military units, Olympians, and professional athletes also engage in some kind of Calisthenics as part of their training. Additionally, teams specifically will engage together as a cohesive unit to enhance connection and discipline. It's similar to what you probably had to do in your regular gym classes growing up.

Example: Lu Xiaojun. This man can snatch 176kg and clean and jerk 204kg, attributing all of his success to Calisthenics. The Olympian said slow, purposeful bodyweight engagement and building is the foundation of his innate strength and success today – not some fancy gym machine.

Why Calisthenics?

Calisthenics is, by every consideration, a "low fuss" form of exercise. In a COVID-19 world, we all need something that is low fuss, low stress, and easy to access. That's why more people than ever before are looking up these kinds of exercises right through social media – it's the primary form of working out.

But, beyond coronavirus and the current situation we find ourselves, we want to go over the pros and cons of this kind of workout engagement, so you are completely aware of what to expect. Let's start with the advantages.

The Advantages of Calisthenics:

1. **Every Person Can Do Calisthenics:** Every single person on the planet, no matter how innately talented, fit, or strong they might be, can do Calisthenics. Everybody is accustomed to performing some kind of bodyweight exercise, whether it's walking up stairs or getting their body out of bed. If a person is elderly, disabled, or overweight, they can still engage in a level of Calisthenics that is right for their body. The resistance can be tailor-made for each individual, as well as the frequency of a particular exercise. If one person can only do ten jumping jacks at a time, that's still Calisthenics. If another person can do 500 at a time, that's still Calisthenics. Even if you can't do a real push-up, you can get on the ground with your knees down and do some variation that engages your body in bodyweight exercise. How amazing is that?

2. **It's Safer Than Gym Equipment:** Do you ever take the time to observe how dangerous gym equipment is? If some of those cables snapped or metal structures broke, people could die. With Calisthenics, it's much, much harder to injure yourself. For starters, none of that fancy gym equipment is lying around anymore. Additionally,

you can only do what your body can support at that given time, which means if you want to try and do upside-down push-ups, if you don't have the strength for it, your body will simply give out. Plus, when you add something like a barbell to a simple workout, you now have the potential of straining or badly pulling your muscles – you are extending beyond your body's own strength ability. With Calisthenics, you can only take what you can take at that given period. It's the safest form of working out, especially for people who are new to the world of exercise.

3. **Workouts Can Be Scaled:** Most people assume that gym equipment is the most efficient way to scale up weights and build muscle. It seems easy – you just add more weight. What people don't realize is that the same concept can be applied to bodyweight exercises. Variations can be made to increase the difficulty of a workout. Additionally, the slower you do a motion, like a push-up, the harder it becomes. Through a focus on quality over quantity, Calisthenics can engage your body in the same kind of weight push-back as gym equipment. Except with Calisthenics, you are actually listening to your body and what it can handle along the way, minimizing injury.

4. **Versatile Strength Results:** Since Calisthenics provides your body with much more than strong muscles, you can transfer those new skills and mind-body connections to other sports, activities, hiking engagements, travels, and so forth. Nearly all calisthenics movements teach the body how to

work in harmony. This ensures that there is a connection between every part of you, increasing coordination, awareness, and flexibility. All of those skills can be used in other sports, activities, traveling, and so forth. It can even make you a more vigilant person if you previously lived your life with your head in the clouds.

5. **Unique Strength Targeting:** Everyone knows about biceps, triceps, quads, and hamstrings, but not everyone knows about the tinier, more important muscles that are also part of your skeletal-muscular system. With Calisthenics, you are making ample use of isometric exercises that isolate certain muscle groups without engaging others. With an isometric exercise, you can push a door in place for one minute. Instead of worrying about the number of reps you are getting in, you are instead holding that one position to activate all of the engaged muscles with precision. More muscles are actually engaged in these kinds of exercises as well, helping those in particular groups to connect and align more seamlessly.

The Disadvantages of Calisthenics:

Nothing is perfect in the world, which is why we have to be honest regarding any possible disadvantages within Calisthenics.

1. **Lower Body Massive Muscle Gain Problems:** When it comes to bodyweight, it can be hard to grow massive quads and hamstrings without outside help. This is because your lower body is built to

It's important to also recognize that not all bodies are the same. Some diets will work for certain body times, while something like the keto diet will work better with others. The secret of the matter is that eating healthy food, vegetables, high protein, low sugars, and drinking lots of water can produce the results you desire.

Please Drink More Water

Did you know that nearly 3/4th of the world lives in a constant state of dehydration? Even though we have more access to processed water today than ever before in human history, we are still living in a state of dehydration. When you are chronically dehydrated, your body is low in energy, dizzy, confusion, unable to focus, unable to feed your cells, irritable, and tired. It can even mess with your sleep cycle, as well as every single organ in your body.

This becomes even worse when you bring training into the mix. Water is used in your boy to carry toxins out, flush out your bloodstream, and deliver nutrients to the cells – which they will need the more you engage in hardcore exercise. Dehydration can impact performance in a major way, preventing your body from getting stronger, strengthening your muscles, and enhancing your mind-body connection. If you don't drink enough water while engaging in Calisthenics, your body will never graduate to the next level.

Most places have readily available drinking water today, so there is really no excuse to be lacking in hydration. A good rule of thumb is to bring a water bottle with you everywhere so you can simply fill it up at a drinking fountain. The more water you drink, the better you will sleep, the more easily you will be able to keep weight off, the more focused you will feel, the more energized you will be while working out, and the more quickly your muscles will be able to rebound after intense periods of exercise.

How much water should you be drinking?
If you weight 75kg, multiply it by 0.033 to arrive at 2.475 liters. Therefore, aiming to drink about 2.5 liters per day should be your goal if you want to maximize the potential of your body. Do keep in mind: if you live in a hot climate or somewhere that causes you to perspire frequently, you may want to increase this figure.

Natural Foods
Not all food is created equal today. Much of the packaged food at grocery stores has been processed so many times, it has been stripped of all natural value and nutrition. It becomes what is known as an empty carb, which is nothing more than glucose weighting to add fat and sluggishness to your body.

Natural food is considered food that has been minimally processed. Basically, this includes all vegetables, fruits, meats, eggs, nuts, or fish. The more natural food you eat, the better you will feel, the more nutrients will be delivered to your cells, and more functioning your digestive system will be. Notice that diary was left out of this chart, as well as processed fats, desserts, and simple carbs.

You don't have to go crazy with your diet and eat strictly plain chicken and spinach every day. As long as you commit to natural foods for every meal and minimize processed foods, you will be providing your body with the nutrients it craves. Be sure to spend extra time ingesting protein, which is what our muscles use to build more muscle after working out.

But won't a natural diet be expensive?
In fact, buying natural foods does not create a more expensive tab than if you were to buy ten boxes of cookies. Think of it as a single-ingredient diet. All you need to do is buy four vegetables, a big thing of chicken, and a carton of eggs to get through a few days. It's a much smaller pantry and shopping list as well.

Bulking It Out
If you desire to gain muscle mass, you need to "eat big to get big." That means you need to pack on the carbs and protein, so your muscles have fuel to get bigger in size. Many bodybuilders will do this for a bulking season and then "cut" the excess fat to lean out. We are not encouraging something this extreme. However, if you want to see serious muscle gains, you will need to be eating in a calorie surplus.

Prioritizing Protein
When it comes to your body, your macronutrients are made up of three categories: proteins, carbohydrates, and fats. Protein is the nutrient responsible for the growth and development of your muscles. The more muscle you have on your body, the more calories your body will burn at complete rest.

Protein can be found in beef, pork, lamb, chicken, egg whites, legumes, nuts, and seeds. You can also use protein powder in your workout shake or just mix it with water. Be sure to have ample amounts of protein in every single meal. Do note: not all protein is created equal. Animal proteins come with a "full amino profile," which means they provide more protein directly into your body than that provided by nuts, etc.

Check the Meat Labels

It's no secret that we are fed meats backed with chemicals and hormones today. It's how they get the biggest yields before the animals are slaughtered. You want to be sourcing grass-fed beef and chicken as opposed to the cheap, factory processed meats. This meat will have more of its original value and protein as well.

What about vegetarians?

There are sources of protein outside of the meat, like yogurt, chickpeas, nuts, and so forth. Although it will be more difficult and more expensive to source your protein this way, do note it is a viable option available to you.

Reduce Your Simple Carb Intake

Your body needs a certain amount of carbs to power through the day. However, these natural or complex carbs, like those found in sweet potatoes, are much more valuable to your body than processed carbs, like white bread. Refined carbs can include pasta, flour, white rice, sugar, pastries, and many desserts. Eating a lot of carbs can not only make it you fatter, but it can also spike your blood sugar, which can lead to increased fat retention, blunted insulin responses, and other undesirable effects – like diabetes. Additionally, many people are developing gluten intolerances today, which means eating these processed carbs can be causing inflammation within your body and slowing down your natural energy.

The best way to get in control of your weight and leanness is to cut all processed carbs from your diet.

Prepare Your Food

As we all know, being stuck with no snacks or eating out at restaurants can be a serious hindrance to any muscle progress. That's why you should be prepping your food in bulk, packing it with you on the go, and eating it when you need it. This can include cooking chicken breasts, brown rice, and broccoli and packing them into five lunch containers for the week. Snacking can be the worst way to get off course as well, which is why having readily available snacks at your disposal can keep you from eating candy bars and potato chips.

There are many recipes out there that show you how to cook in bulk; most of them are free right online. Picking options that are packed with nutrients and low in saturated fats are your best bet. You can pack in bulk by cooking and packing simply one afternoon every week. You can even freeze the items you plan to eat the next week.

What Does the Perfect Diet Look Like?

Again, different diets are suitable for different people. But, we are going to provide a sample diet that should, generally, work for anyone and help them see the callisthenic results they desire. The daily intake is as follows:

- **Breakfast:** Cook two to three eggs (or egg whites for women wanting to cut out fat levels) in a pan.

Add in some spinach and other vegetables to give it some texture. You can also add some lactose-free milk or almond mix for scrambled eggs. Be sure to have a tall glass of water with the meal – no milk. After that, pack snacks of raw veggies and hummus, nuts, and fruit slices to snack on throughout the morning.

- **Lunch:** Time to bring out that bulk meal. This can be tuna salad, chicken salad, beef stew, etc. Be sure to only buy whole wheat bread and stay away from any white bread. Be sure to have a lot of vegetables packed in with a protein source, like a salad with extra chicken breast added to it. Afternoon snacks are the same as breakfast snacks.
- **Dinner:** The last mean of the day can be another bulk meal, like chicken breast with peanut butter and sweet potatoes, peas, asparagus, broccoli. Etc.

Don't forget about the 80/20 rule we mentioned before. If you can't quite practice your Calisthenics six times per week, but rather three times per week, you can make up for it by eating well since diet is 80% of your results. This can be both: a blessing and a curse.

Now that you know how to nourish your body, it's time to learn more about resting and recovery.

Chapter 3: Rest and Recovery

When you are training, jumping, running, and sweating, you are actually not making your body stronger or fitter. That feeling of exhausting is micro-breaks in your muscle fiber as you push your body past its limits. In fact, it's the period of rest and recovery that most directly impacts how strong and stable you will become.

Your body becomes stronger in the intervals between training sessions. Therefore, your body needs a chance to recover. Your body is a beautiful, adaptive organism that can do almost anything if you just give it a moment to rest. And this moment needs to be more than an hour pause between sets. It needs to be proper nutrition, adequate rest, lots of sleep, and of course, lots of water.

First, let's look at how important sleep is for your body.

Bring On the Sleep

There is nothing more important for recovery than sleeping. Most people in the modern world, along with being dehydrated, are also sleep deprived. There are tons of studies that show if the body doesn't receive ample time at night to repair itself or if your sleep is interrupted, your muscles will not be able to repair themselves and grow in strength.

The problem is that stress from life, finances, family, or coronavirus can impact your sleep right now. Be sure to try and power down at night, turn off the news, and turn off your phone when you go to sleep. The blue light emitted from our phones can impact our sleeping ability and trick your body into thinking the sun is coming up again.

For adults, 7-9 hours of sleep per night is recommended for body recovery. If you are recovering after serious physical activity during the day, you might need even more sleep than the recommended 7-hours.

Rest Cycles

The beauty of Calisthenics is that you can control which muscle groups you are activating during your workouts. If you choose to engage your core and lower body muscles one day, you can switch off and work your upper body/back the next day.

It is recommended to get at least one day of rest before attempting to train a similar muscle group again. The general rule is a minimum of 48 hours to recover with a full recovery seen at the 72-96 hour mark post-workout.

Your body needs time to repair those tears in your muscles. While it is repairing those tears, your muscles are getting stronger and more robust. Therefore, making time to actually slow down and rest will make you stronger than ever before. You can switch off muscle groups, as well as take an all-around break from working out every 3-4 days or so. You do not have to work out every single day in a row to see the results you desire.

Why Rest is Particularly Important for Calisthenics

Calisthenics places demand on parts of the body that aren't normally activated by just simply lifting weights. You will feel stress in the elbows, wrists, shoulders, and ligaments, plus your tendons and connective tissues.

These tissues will take much longer to repair themselves than regular muscle tissue.

If you are regularly practicing Calisthenics, then you will need to listen to your body with regards to rest. If it is telling you one day to lay off the exercises, listen to what it is saying to you. You will start to notice when you are pushing your body too far and creating these needed rest periods so you can avoid this kind of overload. It's called "digging too far."

Why Don't We Rest?

Although now reading this, you know how important it is to rest, here are a few reasons why we fail to rest on a daily basis:

- You have yourself convinced you will lose strength, muscle size, or developments in your physical physique if you take a break.
- You want to improve where you currently are, so you're not afraid to go above and beyond to make it happen.
- You're addicted to working out and training your body.
- You have a competition coming up, and you want to make sure you can hit all the marks.

It's important to know you won't lose strength in one week. In fact, by resting and pairing it with proper nutrition, you will gain strength by giving your body some time to relax. Have you ever noticed you can run a mile much more quickly if you do it one day after completely resting, as opposed to after a day at the gym?

Your muscular and neural systems need time to recover and adapt to the workouts you are putting them through. Especially if you are new to the world of Calisthenics, listen to your body and allow it to play catch up.

Planned Workout Weeks

In the coming chapters, we'll explore specific kinds of calisthenics workouts, as well as which ones are right for you and your schedule. We will also explore how you can "load heavier ones" into certain weeks, with less challenging workouts in other weeks. Cycling your engagement is your best move for enhancing your strength while working with your body's natural abilities.

Chapter 4: The Perfect Execution

Don't dream of winning. Train for it.

Without diving too deeply into the scientific world and getting all technical, let's look at what perfect execution means in the lens of Calisthenics. This is a new kind of working out that you are just getting used to, which is why we want you to know more about how to do it perfectly the first time around. Here are some important things to note.

Changing Your Body Angle

You can engage in what is known as "progressions" with simple workouts. With a push-up, you can do it with your knees on the ground, and then graduate to no knees, and then graduate to elevating your feet about your head while you do a push-up.

As you extend the body from a tuck position to a straddle position with push-ups, you can exercise your muscles more aggressively. You start to use the bones as levers, with your joints acting as fulcrums, and your muscles there to apply force. This shifting can move the center of mass from the body further away from the shoulder by straightening the body. This can increase the torque force on your shoulder, especially if you elevate your feet, and so forth.

Resting Length

Muscles are their strongest when they are at their resting length. At this point, the maximum number of cross-bridges can be formed. A cross-bridge is when a contractile component of the muscle – myosin and actin – overlap, with the myosin pulling against the actin to contract the muscle. So, if you shorten or lengthen the muscle when a lighter load is placed on the body, you can stimulate an adaption as if you were using a heavier weight.

Training Concepts

It's important to know the following definitions when building out your calisthenics routine:

- Repetitions: Often shortened to reps, the number of reps you can perform in a single set can define the intensity of the workout. You can do ten push-ups in a row before resting, completing a single set.
- Sets: The number of reps you can do in one session is known as a set. The more sets you do, the more difficult a workout can become. It is common to do ten reps, three times, for three sets.
- Rests: This is the amount of time taken to rest in-between activating the muscles. There are short rest periods and long rest periods.
- Tempo: This is the speed at which you do your repetitions. This can be common in "high-intensity interval training" when the person aims to do as many reps of one exercise in 60-seconds as possible.
- Load: This is the intensity of the workout; i.e., you can create a heavier load in Calisthenics by lifting your feet above the angle of your head during an arm workout.
- Volume: The number of exercises performed in a single workout.

Understanding Repetition vs. Strength
There is a repetition continuum that exists in the world of Calisthenics. It shows strength at one end and endurance at the other end. The strength side is attained through low repetitions and heavier weights, with slower tempos. The endurance side is less weight with more repetitions or a greater tempo. Therefore, you should understand the following:

- You cannot build strength and endurance in one singular workout. You need to curate a schedule that prioritizes both.
- Spending time enhancing your strength will enhance your endurance and vice versa.
- Strength takes longer to develop than basic endurance conditioning.

Quality vs. Quantity

Quality is ALWAYS more important than quantity in Calisthenics. These are exercises that are specifically engaging in numerous muscles, tendons, and even your nervous system altogether. It's not about brute force, massive weights, or showing off; it's about engaging your entire body in an effective workout that has been used for thousands of years.

Therefore, get the idea of "number of reps" out of your head. In fact, many times, these workouts can be even harder if you do just one rep (a squat), and hold it for 60-seconds.

As mentioned above, the best way to enhance your strength is to engage in isometric exercises. Doing reps in a slow and steady manner, working your way around your body at a quality speed, is how you are going to see the most results in the shortest amount of time. Leave the quantity obsession at the gym.

Systemized Resting

Your body is a mesmerizing machine with hundreds of different moving parts. If you engage some of those moving parts (muscles the day before), it's possible to allow them to rest the next day if you target another group of parts that were otherwise left un-stimulated during that workout.

We have already mentioned this, which is why you now understand everything you need to know about perfect execution in the world of Calisthenics.

Chapter 5: How to Build Muscles

We're going to take a moment in this chapter to cover the basics related to building muscle and "getting shred." It's important to understand exactly how muscle is built in your body, so you can better adhere to what your body needs during your callisthenic workouts.

Some of these things we have already touched on, so we'll make this a brief list.

The 6 Basics of Building Muscle

1. **More Protein, More Meat:** Your muscle's number one source of growth and development is protein. It's not carbs or fat. It's protein, which means if you want to build more muscle, you need to seriously ramp up the amount of protein you are eating. As we have mentioned, animal protein is your best, natural source of protein available today.
2. **Eat More:** You need to be in a calorie surplus to grow your muscles today. You can use this formula to calculate the proper amount of calories for your muscle growth: take your weight, multiple it by 12 to get your caloric intake need. Then multiply that by 1.6 to estimate your resting metabolic rate.
3. **Big Muscle Groups:** For the beginners out there, working on the biggest muscle groups, like quads, chest, back, and shoulders, can produce the quickest results for you. These are muscles that want to swell in size, which is why squats, deadlifts, bent-over rows, bench presses, and so forth are great ways to get these muscles swelling. Of

course, you can do all of these without any gym equipment, but rather, just your bodyweight.

4. **Protein Shakes:** In a 2001 study at the University of Texas, it was found that lifters who drank a protein shake with amino acids and carbs, right before working out, performed better throughout the workout. It was even more effective than those who had their shakes after the workout.
5. **Take Breaks:** That's right; taking breaks from working out is one of the most effective weighs to build huge muscles. If you can, take breaks every few days from your Calisthenics and be sure to target different muscle groups every other day.
6. **Eat Throughout the Day:** Eating every three-hours is an effective way to build muscle over-time. When you workout, your body is going to require new energy afterward, which is why supply it with the nutrients it desires throughout the entire day is going to help you see the results you want to see.

Listen to Your Body

Obviously, there are differences in men versus women for muscle building, as well as different body types. If you are overweight and exploring Calisthenics, then working to shed fat might be more important to you than building muscle. Or, if you are skinny with zero muscle tone, then light workouts might be all you need to start seeing results. Listen to your body.

If you feel plain Calisthenics has made your lower body hit a muscular plateau, consider progressing your movements.

Chapter 6: Workout Equipment

As we have mentioned, it is entirely possible to engage your body in calisthenics workouts without equipment. In fact, that's the whole point of this kind of bodyweight training. You are already equipped with everything you need to get into top physical fitness.

However, even in ancient Greek times, humans figured out if they pushed rocks, climbed trees, pulled themselves up onto things, etc., they could enhance their physical fitness. Therefore, there are some very simple equipment items you can consider for your calisthenics makeover, most of which can be kept right at home.

First, let's look at some generic equipment. After that, we'll divide them into difficulty rankings, so you have a better idea of what is right for you.

Callisthenic Equipment to Consider

- **The Pull-Up Bar:** Although this isn't necessarily a staple for your callisthenic workout at home, it can be a valuable possibility to challenge your body and push your boundaries. A pull-up bar can be bought on Amazon for little-to-nothing and mounted in the home with few tools. Not only can this pull-up bar now be used for pulling exercises, but it can also be used for hanging and core exercises. That's what makes this item the most cost-effective piece of calisthenics equipment you could be buying today. Just because you can't do a pull-up, doesn't mean it can't be valuable to your training routine. Remember: if you cannot afford a pull-up bar, you can find equivalents at local playgrounds in your town.

- **Dip Bars:** Next, we have the dip bar, which enables a person to place both hands at a bar at their waist level and dip up and down to engage, namely, the triceps. Dip bars can appear in a lot of variations, with different thicknesses, widths, and heights. You will want to find one that is right for your height, as buying one too low to the ground will make it hard to physically dip repeatedly. You can place a set of dip bars in your back yard, basement, or again, go find them at the local playground.
- **Parallettes:** Similar to the dip bar, parallettes are two bars that are set a certain amount of feet apart facing the same way. Much more portable and lower to the ground than the dup bar, parallettes are made for pushing exercises, like a push-up, handstand, planche work, etc. Since they are separate units, you can change how far apart they are to make certain workouts more or less challenging. This can help you take a push up to the next level if you want to be able to dip lower than your body before coming back into a planking position.

  Parallettes come in different types and options today. Be sure to buy some that are sturdy enough to hold your bodyweight. You will also have to find ones that have a bar thickness that is comfortable for your grip depending upon your hand size. If you need to save money, you can even make your own. We recommend checking out information YouTube videos to make this happen. Typically, a thick dowel is all you will need and some wood.

- **Clothing:** You can purposely wear more clothing to get your body sweating while you are working out. However, the purpose of Calisthenics is to allow your body full range of motion, which is why light and nimble clothing is preferred. But, there are ankle weights, wrist weights, and plenty of sweatshirts you can pack on if you want to turn our workout into more of a cardio burnout.
- **Chalk:** Many of these bars you are going to be holding and pulling will require a strong and sturdy grip. As all the gymnasts use in their competitions, chalk can be an easy way to ensure you have a firm grip on the bars. With a firm grip, you can focus more on your body, mind, and wrist connection, which means you will be able to hold the exercises for longer. You can consider buying traditional powdered chalk available in square blogs; you can also buy liquid chalk that comes in a small bottle.
- **Foam Roller:** Foam rollers are all the rage today as they are an excellent way to massage out fascia and muscles in the body. A foam roller is used for self-myofascial release, which is a great way to activate your muscles before working out, as well as cool them down when you are done. Foam rollers are a great way to get rid of any sore parts, scar tissue, and knots in the muscle fibers. You can buy them for affordable rates on any eCommerce site.

- **Training Partners:** As you can imagine, adding a training partner into the mix can help you take a variety of bodyweight exercises to the next level. A training partner is a great way to not only extend what you are able to do at home, but it can also be a great way to stay motivated to work out more than before. A partner will also be able to observe you working out and provide any real-time feedback to help with your form and performance.

That completes the kind of equipment you can use in a calisthenics workout regime. Next, let's look at what you should be aiming to do as a beginner, intermediate, and professional athlete.

Beginners

As a beginner in Calisthenics, you are going to craft an entire workout plan with zero equipment. Equipment only increases the difficulty of these exercises, which is why you won't need to even entertain the thought of doing pull-ups without any assistance. In the next chapter, we'll outline how the perfect workout plan for you looks like.

Of course, a foam roller for recovery is always a good idea, even as a beginner.

Intermediates

When you reach the intermediate calisthenics workout label, which can occur around the two to the three-month mark, you might want to start increasing the difficulty of your workouts. This is a great time to bring on partners who can help you fine-tune your form, as well as invest in basic equipment like the pull-up bar and the dip bars. You don't need to get too crazy yet – these bars will provide you with plenty of challenges.

Pros

At the pro callisthenic mark, which is generally after one-year of intense calisthenics training and engagement, you are ready to bring on the parallettes, as well as the chalk. You are also ready to explore the most challenging parks of a local playground. Please do not advance to this level after spending many months strengthening your body, core, and balance. Although Calisthenics is relatively safe, exploring playgrounds and suspending yourself 10-feet off the ground can make this kind of working out dangerous.

Chapter 7: The Perfect Workout Plan

'The best view comes after the hardest climb.'

When it's time to finally put this all into practice and make a workout plan that is best for you, the very first thing you will want to consider is the location of your exercise. This is a big choice because if you do not find a suitable location, you will be less likely to really push your boundaries with calisthenics training.

Obviously, gyms and training centers, during normal times in human history, can be acceptable. However, while we are at home, that means you will want to clear a space in your house that can be suitable. The best bet is usually a basement with lots of space and flat surfaces. If you are in an apartment, clear out space in the living room or your bedroom, possibly requiring yourself to push furniture against the wall. You will also want to invest in some kind of yoga mat you can use for your joints when you are on the ground.

Naturally, you can train outside as well. With the warmer months coming, parks and playgrounds can be a viable option for engaging your body without attending the gym. Many playgrounds have options for pull-up bars, dip bars, monkey bars, poles, and ropes. However, please check with your local authorities and ensure you are not breaking any social distancing mandates by going to the playground and working out today.

Of course, feel free to join callisthenic social media groups where you can learn more about options in your area. There might be outdoor, open spaces with obstacles that are already set up for this kind of activity.

Although we can't provide special workout plans for every single person in the world within this e-book, we can dive into what is regarded as a beginner's guide to curating a calisthenics workout. Let's check it out below.

Beginner's Calisthenics Sample Workout Guide

Day 1:

- **Planking: hold it for 30-60 seconds and then rest.**
- **8 squats**
- **8 lunges**
- **8 push-ups**
- **8 laying down leg raises**
- **20 mountain climbers per leg**
- **8 push-ups to round it all out**

Day 2:

- **5 leg raises**
- **15 deadlifts**
- **9 jump squats**
- **15 squats**
- **10 calf raises**
- **15 burpees**

Day 3: REST DAY

Day 4:

- 20 wide push-ups
- 20 mountain climbers
- 60-second wall sit
- 15 clap push-ups
- 30 squats
- 60-second plank
- 30-second superman hold

Day 5:

- 100-meter run
- 10 push-ups
- 45-second jumping jacks
- 30-second alternating high knees
- 30-second mountain climbers
- 15-second plank

Day 6: HIIT Day

- 15-second sprint
- 45-second walk
- Repeat 4 times
- 30-second sprint
- 45-second walk
- Repeat 4 times
- 15-second sprint
- 45-second walk
- Repeat 4 times

Day 7: REST DAY

Workout Plans for Specific Goals

1. **Building Muscles:** The body is an amazing modern feat, which is why you will need to engage in different kinds of workouts to yield different desired results. As we have covered in an entire chapter, for building muscle, you will need to engage in hard, heavy lifting, working out, and calorie surpluses. You will need to consume lots of protein and work to bulk up your body and feed your muscle gain. This is often desired by men, bodybuilders, or women looking to compete in competitions. Please always take caution when lifting with heavy weights or engaging in intense workouts to follow instructions and keep your body safe.

2. **Losing Weight:** If you're number one goal is to lose weight from working out, then you are going to want to curate a schedule that balances cardio fitness with weight training. Why? Weight training helps your body to build muscle, which has a higher resting caloric burning rate than normal cells or fat in your body. Additionally, pairing that muscle with cardiovascular exercise is a popular method for "cutting" when it comes to bodybuilders.

   The sample beginner's workout provided above is a great starting point for shedding weight from your Calisthenics. In this case, you will not want to be in a calorie surplus, but rather, engaging in a slight calorie deficit. However, when anyone works out, they need to provide their body with nutrients. Starvation is not the answer. So eating more vegetables and fruits as opposed to carbs is a great way to bring your caloric intake down while also feeding your body simultaneously.

3. **Shedding Stubborn Belly Fat:** It is a myth that you can specifically target belly f fat on your body and nothing else. Belly fat is a result of a bodyweight fat surplus, which is why to lose fat on your stomach, you will have to lose fat elsewhere. Some of the following solutions will help you target your overall fat surplus: avoid most, if not all, sugary foods; do more cardio exercises than you were previously doing; cut back on carbs, especially processed carbs; cut alcohol out of your diet altogether; avoid foods that have trans fats in them; reduce your stress levels – yes, stress can contribute not only to stubborn fat gain but especially fat gain in your gut region; and lastly, switch to a high protein diet.

   Engaging in abdominal exercises as part of your Calisthenics is a great way to tone your stomach region while also improving your stability and balance. Your core is the center of your body, which means a stronger core will make you more athletic and agile in all of your exercises.

4. **Improving Stamina and Endurance:** As we have mentioned, stamina and endurance sit on one end of a spectrum while strength sits on another. You can't improve both at the same time.

Therefore, although you will spend some part of your week, making your muscles stronger and more toned, you will want to spend 2-3 days targeting your endurance and cardio tolerance. One great way is through cycled sprints, as listed in the previous chapter, as well as high interval intensity training. Never forget: your body is not a never-ending battery. It needs time to rest, which is why improving stamina will take some rest days and time. Practice makes perfect, so give your body time to adjust.

5. **Improving Agility and Flexibility:** Agility is the ability to move quickly and easily with a nimbleness that is effortless. An agile person can maneuver around obstacles without any issues, shifting the balance from side to side with isolated movement skills that can include coordination, speed, reflexes, balance, strength, and endurance. Calisthenics is the best way to develop your personal agility and flexibility through isometric movements, holds, and progressions.

   Therefore, exercises that involve pull-up bars, dip bars, parallettes, etc., as well as holds during these exercises, slow, purposeful movements, and so forth, will enhance your body's mind-muscle connection. As you train your nervous system through Calisthenics, you will become more agile in the process.

   As for flexibility, this can be improved in two ways: stretching pre and post-workout, and engaging in yoga. Yoga allows your body to move through a range of motion, and although it may be uncomfortable at the time, holding those specific poses – that have been used for thousands of years – will allow your muscles and joints to open up and lengthen in size. As a person ages, their flexibility decreases, which is why starting the practice of yoga on a weekly basis right now is something you will not regret.

And with that, we have concluded everything you need to know about calisthenics 101, as well as how to live a healthier, more active, and fitness-modeled lifestyle today.

Conclusion

Humans have a tendency today to take something simple and proven and make it more complex. We'd rather sign up for specialized barber packages through our computers than just walk down the street, into a barbershop, and sit down. The same thing has happened to exercise, fitness, and nutrition. There are all of these "fad diets" and "special workout machines" that promise to help people build muscle and shed weight fast.

If that was the case, wouldn't everyone own those machines?

Calisthenics has been with humans since before history textbooks. It's one of the most innate, powerful, and beneficial ways to engage more than just your muscles – it's a way to wake up your entire body, fascia, nervous system, mind-body connections, and even your soul.

We hope you have enjoyed reading along with us here and learning more about how you can get in control of your life – even during social distancing. Calisthenics has proven to be an effective way to stay fit without leaving your home or apartment, which is something all of us need access to today, if not for our physical health, then for our mental health.

Please feel free to reach out with any feedback or commentary. We'd love to know your thoughts and what you have taken away from this read.

Cheers!

Imprint

- Author: Talha Erol
- Address: Birkenstr.2, 64747 Breuberg, Germany
- Email: tarol@protonmail.com

Printed in Poland
by Amazon Fulfillment
Poland Sp. z o.o., Wrocław

60330725R00028